Meet...
NED KELLY

WRITTEN BY JANEEN BRIAN
ILLUSTRATED BY MATT ADAMS

RANDOM HOUSE AUSTRALIA

To Max Colwell, a dear friend who always brought history to life. JB

To my family. MA

A Random House book
Published by Random House Australia Pty Ltd
Level 3, 100 Pacific Highway, North Sydney NSW 2060
www.randomhouse.com.au

This edition published by Random House Australia in 2014

Addresses for companies within the Random House Group can be found at
www.randomhouse.com.au/offices

National Library of Australia
Cataloguing-in-Publication Entry

Author: Brian, Janeen
Title: Meet Ned Kelly / Janeen Brian; Matt Adams, illustrator.
ISBN: 978 1 74275 719 3 (pbk.)
Subjects: Kelly, Ned, 1855–1880 – Juvenile literature.
Bushrangers – Australia – Juvenile literature.
Other Authors/Contributors: Adams, Matt
Dewey Number: 364.155092

Cover and internal illustrations © Matt Adams
Back cover illustration of old poster © Pablo H Caridad/Shutterstock.com
Internal parchment background © MaxyM/Shutterstock.com
Cover and internal design by Kirby Armstrong
Typeset by Kirby Armstrong
Printed and bound in China through Asia Pacific Offset Ltd

Ned Kelly was born in 1854 in Beveridge, Victoria. When Ned was a boy his father died and the family struggled to get by.

This is the story of how Ned Kelly became Australia's most famous bushranger.

Ned Kelly went to school for a year or two.
He had books and friends and fun.
But that all changed when his father died.
He became a widow's son.

The family was poor. They had to move
to a farm that was nothing grand.
Ned soon learnt that **those in charge
took all the good, rich land.**

Ned loved his family and was brave.
He had a sash he wore with pride.
A reward it was for saving a mate
from a creek running fast and wide.

Times were tough as Ned grew up,
and police were often near.
They picked on Ned and his family,
though it was clear Ned held no fear.

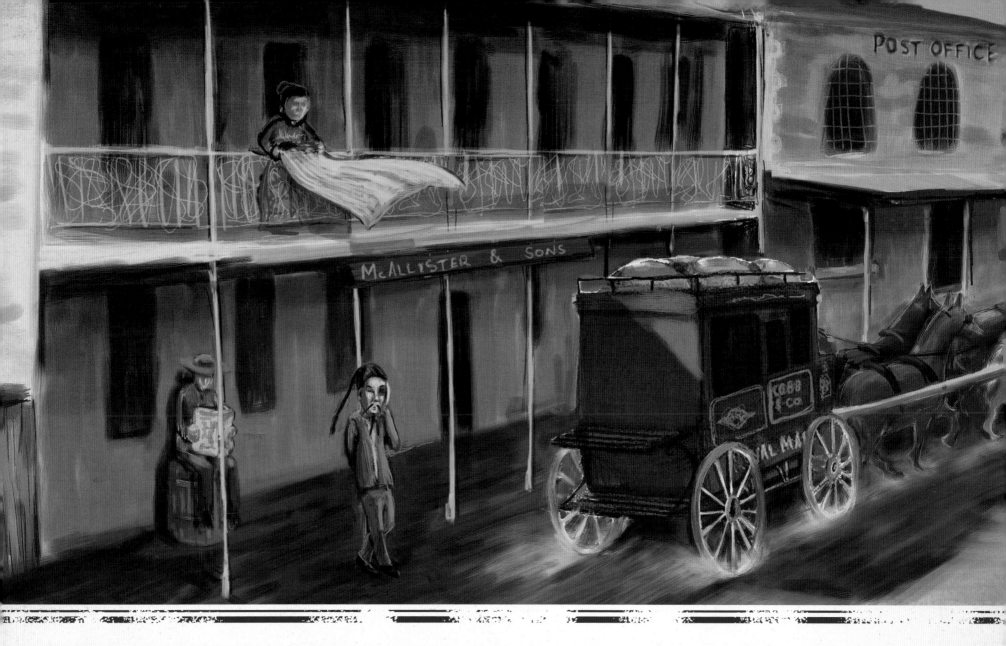

Ned was fair, but had hit a man
and helped an outlaw on the run.
Police wanted him for crimes like these,
and sometimes even for none.

Then Ned helped a friend by swapping a horse.
It was stolen **but Ned didn't know.**
Ned was arrested for having that horse,
but the friend was soon free to go.

Ned was gaoled for three long years.
He was nineteen when he got out.
By then Ned's horses had all been sold.
'It was the police,' Ned said. 'I've no doubt.'

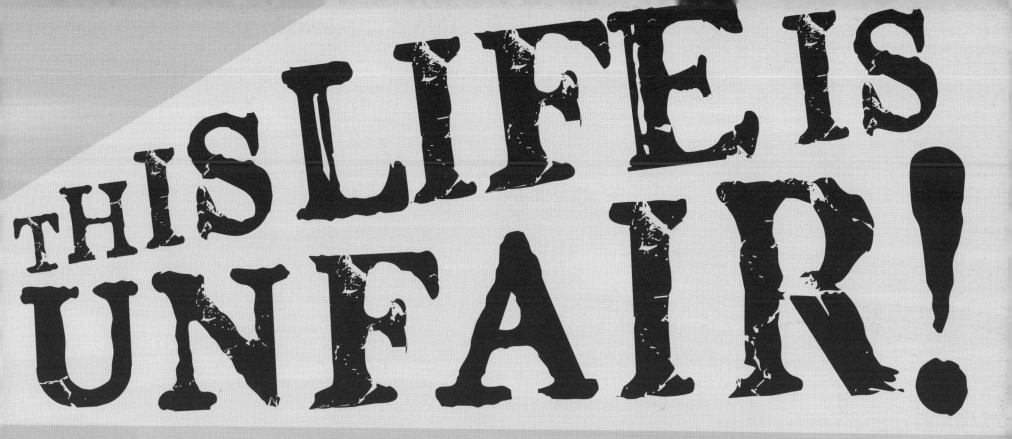

THIS LIFE IS UNFAIR!

Ned cried when released.
'Police are drunk or they're greedy.
There's **NO JUSTICE** from landlords, nor from the law,
to help out the poor or the needy.'

Ned saddled his horse and rode far away.
Soon a policeman came after Ned's brother.
'But he hasn't been stealing,' Ellen Kelly yelled.
So the policeman arrested their mother.

Ned's mother was gaoled.
Her baby as well.
Dan left and Ned hid to stay free.
He'd heard that the policeman had
lied to the judge, saying,
'NED KELLY TRIED
TO KILL ME.'

Ned grew wild when he heard **and his heart almost broke**
to think of his mother so sad.
He joined brother Dan and two mates in the bush,
hatched a plan that later turned bad.

Police moved fast to hunt Ned Kelly down.
His friends warned, 'Watch where you go.'
Ned said to his mates, 'We'll outwit the police
or they'll shoot me straight off, that I know.'

'We'll ride to their camp at Stringybark Creek.
Take their horses and guns and then go.'
But when Ned called 'BAIL UP!' a policeman took aim.
So Ned shot him in one single blow.

Two other policemen were killed in the battle.
The gang were now outlaws in danger.
Rewards were set up for their capture or death.
NED KELLY WAS NOW A BUSHRANGER.

Ned and his gang **robbed the bank** at Euroa,
though none of the men hurt the staff.
A bank teller mentioned that Ned was polite,
did horse-riding tricks for a laugh.

'I've become a **FORCED OUTLAW,** Ned always said.
'I'll harm none that doesn't harm me.
But I hate those who bully and who are unjust.
And there are more 'round these parts who agree.'

For more than a year
NED'S GANG
WANDERED
FREE,
although Ned was
always on guard.
In a letter he said
'us folk who are poor
find colonial life
very hard.'

But Ned had good friends who knew his hard times.
They helped him in every way.
The months soon passed by. The gang wasn't caught.
The reward got BIGGER each day.

Police were fed up and so came an order
for hundreds to catch Ned and his men.
Ned needed a plan to stop those police.
Yet what could he do? HOW? And wHEN?

Then came more news that was just as grim.
A mate had lied, been untrue.
'He's betrayed us all,' Ned said to his gang.
'Told police where we are, what we do.

We'll get rid of the **traitor**. That'll bring the police.
Then we can get rid of them too.
After that there's a chance for us to live free.
So listen, boys, here's what we'll do.'

Ned gathered up those who lived 'round Glenrowan,
locked them up one and all at the inn.
'I'm not going to hurt you,' Ned said to them,
'but I don't want a fuss or a din.'

The police were headed to Glenrowan by train.
'Pull the tracks up!' Ned cried. 'Make it quick!'
Then the gang fixed their guns and settled to wait
for police to walk into their trick.

A hostage talked Ned into letting him go.
'Leave now,' Ned said. 'Walk off in peace.'
The man rode away, flagged down the train
and in that way saved the police.

A standoff began, which lasted for hours.
NED ESCAPED to warn friends of the danger.

At dawn he returned in an outfit of metal. AN IRON-CLAD, EERIE BUSHRANGER.

The armour protected Ned's arms, head and waist.
The bullets bounced off one by one.
Sergeant Steele took a shot at Ned's legs that were bare.
With a cry, Ned collapsed and was done.

Beneath that thick metal was Ned's long green sash.
He'd worn it once more with great **pride**.
He was then led away by police from the inn,
from the place where his **loyal** mates died.

'Ned Kelly, you are GUILTY of murder!' said the judge.

Our Ned was but twenty-five years old.

In the spring he was hung in the Old Melbourne Gaol.

But his story is still being told.

TIMELINE

- **1820**: John 'Red' Kelly is born in County Tipperary, Ireland.

- **1832**: Ellen Quinn is born in County Antrim, Ireland.

- **1840**: John Kelly is transported to Australia as a convict to serve seven years for stealing two pigs.

- **1841**: The Quinn family emigrates to Victoria, Australia.

- **1850**: John Kelly and Ellen Quinn meet and are married by November.

- **1853**: John Kelly travels alone to the goldfields and makes money to buy a farm near Beveridge in Victoria.

- **1853**: John and Ellen Kelly's first child, Annie, is born.

- **1854** (December): Edward 'Ned' Kelly is born.

- **1857**: Margaret 'Maggie' Kelly is born.

- **1859**: James Kelly is born.

- **1861**: Daniel 'Dan' Kelly is born. He will later join Ned as a member of the Kelly Gang.

- **1863**: Catherine 'Kate' Kelly is born.

- **1864**: The Kelly family sell their farm in Beveridge and move to a rented farm near Avenel, Victoria.

- **1865**: 11-year-old Ned risks his life to save a younger boy, Richard Shelton, from drowning in Hughes Creek near Avenel.

- **1865**: John Kelly is sent to gaol for four months for cattle stealing.

- **1865**: Grace Kelly is born.

- **1866**: John Kelly dies of Dropsy. Ned is forced to leave school to help support the family.

- **1867**: Ellen Kelly and her children move to a farm at Eleven Mile Creek in Victoria.

- **1869**: Ned is arrested for robbing and hitting a Chinese merchant, Ah Fook, but there is not enough proof to send him to gaol.

- **1870** (May): Ned is arrested again and held in custody for helping a bushranger called Harry Power. Ned is later cleared of this charge.

☞ **1870** (October): Ned and his uncle Jack Lloyd get into a fight with a travelling salesman. Ned is sentenced to six months' hard labour.

☞ **1871**: Three weeks after Ned's release from gaol he is arrested for receiving a stolen horse and is sentenced to three years' hard labour.

☞ **1874**: Ned's mother marries George King.

☞ **1874**: Ned is released from gaol and discovers that the police have sold nearly all his horses.

☞ **1878** (April): Constable Alexander Fitzpatrick visits the Kelly homestead to arrest Ned's brother, Dan, for cattle rustling. A fight breaks out and Constable Fitzpatrick is injured. Dan escapes, and the constable arrests Ned's mother instead. Ned, Dan and two mates, Steve Hart and Joe Byrne, go on the run.

☞ **1878** (October): Ned and his mates kill three policemen during a shootout at Stringybark Creek. Ned, Dan, Steve and Joe are now outlaws and become known as the Kelly Gang.

☞ **1878** (December): After the gang raid a bank at Euroa, the Government offers a £2500 reward for their capture.

☞ **1879** (February): The Kelly Gang rob a bank at Jerilderie.

☞ **1880** (26 June): Joe Byrne shoots a man named Aaron Sherritt for betraying the gang to the police.

☞ **1880** (27 June): The police hear about the murder of Aaron Sherritt. They send a special police train carrying 200 officers to Beechworth, via Glenrowan, to hunt down the Kelly Gang.

☞ **1880** (27 June): The Kelly Gang take 60 hostages at the Glenrowan Inn. Ned orders the rail tracks to be ripped up to derail the special police train.

☞ **1880** (27–28 June): Ned allows Thomas Curnow, a local schoolteacher, to leave the inn to care for his sick wife. But Curnow alerts the police and saves their train from derailing.

☞ **1880**: (28 June): Siege at Glenrown Inn, followed by a long gun battle between the police and the Kelly Gang. The inn is burnt to the ground, and Dan Kelly, Steve Hart and Joe Byrne are killed. Ned Kelly fights on in a suit of armour until he is eventually injured and arrested.

☞ **1880** (11 November): Ned Kelly is hanged in the Old Melbourne Gaol.

Also in the *Meet*... series

And look out for more great *Meet*... books coming soon